# Who Needs Nappies? Not Me!

Justine Avery

illustrated by Seema Amjad

SUTEKI CREATIVE

# Who needs nappies?

Not Me!

For
—and partly crafted by—
the girl who can move mountains,
when empowered by a great chant.

—J.A.

For all the children
of the world.

—S.A.

**Justine Avery** is an award-winning author who loves writing stories for all sorts of readers. She was born in America but grew up—and is still growing up—all over the world as a natural explorer with a curiosity for all things. She's jumped out of airplanes, off of very high bridges, and into shark-infested waters—to name a few adventures. And books are her favorite adventures of all.

**Seema Amjad** is a digital artist and book illustrator from the mountainous Hunza Valley in the Himalayas.

First published 2021 by Suteki Creative

FIRST EDITION

Copyright © 2021 Justine Avery
Illustrated by Seema Amjad
All rights reserved.

In accordance with international copyright law, this publication, in full or in part, may not be scanned, copied, stored in a retrieval system, duplicated, reproduced, uploaded, transmitted, resold, or distributed online or offline—in any form or by any means—without prior, explicit permission of the author.

But *please do*… lend this book freely! It's *yours*—you own it. So, pass it on, trade it in, exchange it with and recommend it to other readers. Books are the very best gifts.

ISBN: 978-1-63882-121-2
ISBN: 978-1-63882-118-2 (ebook)
ISBN: 978-1-63882-120-5 (paperback)
ISBN: 978-1-63882-123-6 (audio book)

# Discover more...

## uniquely wonderful, utterly imaginative children's books by Justine Avery.

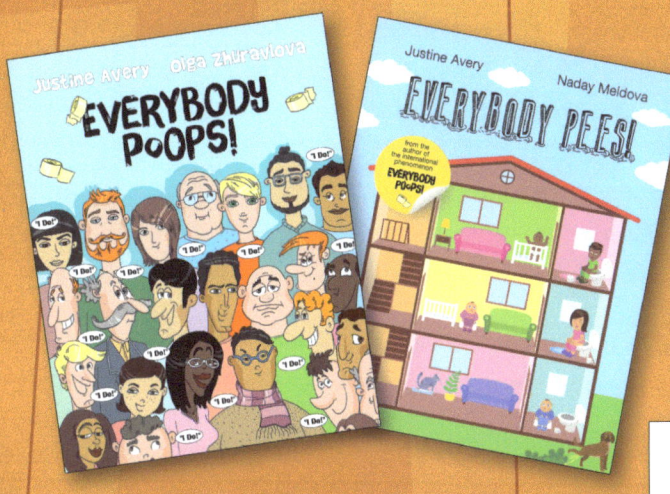
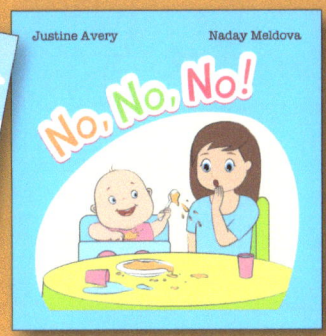
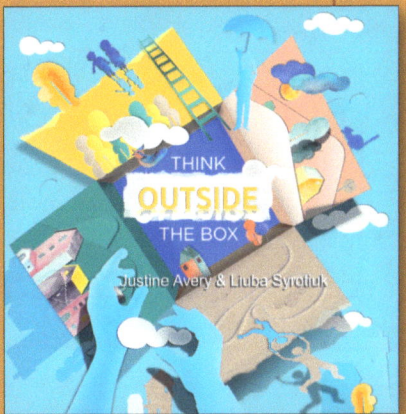

**Join in the fun!**
Visit JustineAvery.com,
and join in all the exclusive
fun and freebies.

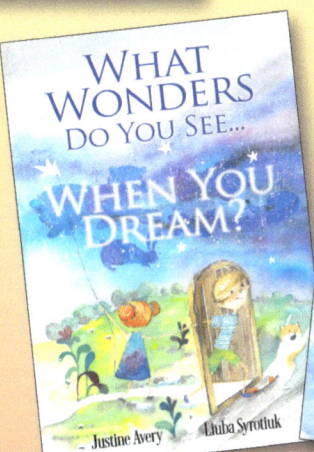
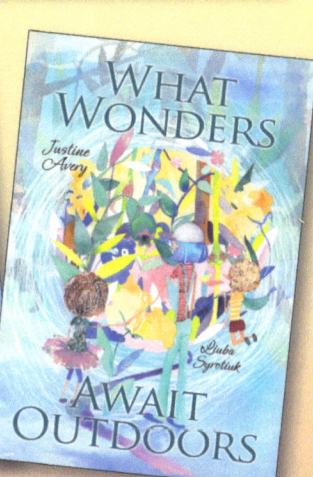